office

SOLITAIRE

Atlin Williams

MINERVA PRESS
WASHINGTON LONDON MONTREUX

SOLITAIRE
Copyright © Atlin Williams 1997

All Rights Reserved

No part of this book may be reproduced in any form,
by photocopying or by any electronic or mechanical means,
including information storage or retrieval systems,
without permission in writing from both the copyright owner
and the publisher of this book.

ISBN 1 86106 190 0

First Published 1997 by
MINERVA PRESS
195 Knightsbridge
London SW7 1RE

Printed in Great Britain by
B.W.D. Ltd, Northolt, Middlesex

SOLITAIRE

*To my daughters
Liane, Philippa and Omotayo,
who gave me so much encouragement.*

Foreword from the Author

I am Atlin Williams, the daughter of Thomas and Mary Williams. I was born in the Parish of St Mary on the 15 December, 1956, in Jamaica.

I came to reside in London in 1966. I was educated at John Kelly Girls' School in North-West London, and in 1988 I studied for a BSc (Hons) Applied Social Science (in information and communication) at the University of North London. On completion of my degree in 1991 I worked as a librarian.

Contents

You	9
Sweet Cool Blackness	11
Farewell	13
Eyes	15
Speak Beyond All Consequences	18
A Scream Within	23
Time You Old Culprit	25
Anticipation	27
Reminiscence	29
Disarray	31
Mixed Feelings	33
Last Resort	36
Dear Lord	38
Band of Gold	40
Feelings	42
Fresh Flowers and a Wreath	44
Boundaries	46
The Blues	48
Gold Coast	50
A Gaze	52

You

Solitaire stands on an empty beach, as the waves lick the
jagged rocks, and the breeze skips past her face.

As she stands there in the dawn, the dew lightly falls on
her head and shoulders, covering her whole body.

She stares into the distance, and sees you coming. To her
delight you are the calm, the gentleness, the smile;
the comfort, her refuge.

Your vision is excellent, yet you are blind. She exists but
you are unaware of her existence. She rubs shoulders with you
daily.

As she stands there, and observes you passing, she thinks of
divulging her untold love to you. Caution stretches out a
cold hand, and in concealment she wraps her body in the darkness
of the dawn.

To her delight you are the calm, the gentleness, the smile;
the comfort and her refuge.

The tender heart agrees the anguish lingers close by. What if transformation could lead Solitaire to the covert of a rock?

In the darkness of the dawn she wishes to be an unfeeling rock which she knows is void of the love, the anguish that she feels.

To her delight you are the calm, the gentleness, the smile;
the comfort and her refuge.

An optimistic element engages in battle with pessimism, and is found to be triumphant. To live is to love, to be alive!

In that instant Solitaire reaches out and parts the dawn, and soars into the day like a phoenix.

To her delight you are the calm, the gentleness, the smile;
the comfort and her refuge.

In her flight of liberty, she is a dove and a hawk at once,
as she clasps the gentleness, the calm, the smile;
and the comfort in her arms.

You and Solitaire are one, in the beauty of your togetherness,
the sun penetrates your fragile bodies, as it projects its
cordial blessings upon your lives.

To her delight you are the calm, the gentleness, the smile;
the comfort and her refuge.

Sweet Cool Blackness

Sweet cool blackness, with your sensuous smile, let me taste your lips of essence, just for a while.

Wrap your beautiful silky blackness, around me, like a concealing cloak. Let me find refuge in your sanctuary, as you whisper cordial and meaningful things to my receptive ears.

I have known too often that the brevity of love is akin to a rose that is fully grown, and in a short space of time withers and dies. I became a dying stalk, which yielded no blossoms.

Sweet cool blackness, with your sensuous smile, let me taste your lips of essence, just for a while.

A state of nothingness prevailed, then one day, the sun which was personified as you, distributed its magnificent rays into the heavens, and kissed the universe.

The thrushes sung their melodious songs, as the doves soared through the azure sky. Weeping willow trees stretched out their mighty branches of pink and white blossoms.

Sweet cool blackness, with your sensuous smile, let me taste your lips of essence, just for a while.

The rain came and saturated everything in sight. Then life, with its splendid spells, shook the withered stalk, and whispered:

To live is to be loved, to be alive, to be alive without someone to love is a waste of the body and soul. Waltz with sweet cool blackness in glee.

Sweet cool blackness, with your sensuous smile, let me taste your lips of essence for all time.

Farewell

A beautiful goddess stood in front of me, her
skin was ebony and her hair was long and dark.
Her nose and mouth were perfectly formed,
Her fingers were intended to play innumerable
instruments as they were long, shapely and
elegantly created.

I loved her dearly and strove to gain her
attention and her affection.

I recollect when she would sit outside of our
house under the palm trees. Very often the sun
danced, kissed and caressed her face, arms
and shoulders while her elegant body held
and supported me in her gentle arms.

Oh! the songs her melodious tones glided into
my receptive ears and created utopia before
I fell asleep without a care for life's trials
and tribulations.

My beautiful goddess fell asleep one blustery
cold day at the beginning of the year when
the snow fell and spread its thick treacherous blanket
on the ground.

The doctors said it was incurable as she went
through the stages of transformation beyond
recognition. Her eyes conveyed to me that
she loved life and did not want to leave
so soon. But alas, we have no control over
our time span on earthly plains.

Farewell for now my dearest goddess.
You are still alive in my heart.

Eyes

I
Why do they reveal so much?
> Be it favourable or unfavourable

They meet and depths are rapidly explored
> without the need to touch.

II
What can you see in the versatile
> Mirrors of my moral, immoral soul?

Can you see love, timelessness, faithfulness,
> Nature, hate, evasiveness? Much

inquisition, why should you care?

III
Favoured by fortune is the person who embraces
> you and searches your wonderfully structured face

With intent to penetrate your eyes. Not with a
> vile instrument. But instead with loving

anticipation of your inner thoughts.
> Has anyone ever kissed and touched your

Precious eyes?

IV

Fool, idiotic is the person who walks through life
  with you hand in hand and neglects to kiss and
tenderly touch your eyes, yearning, burning
  utterances appear immaterial when it can all
be said through the mirrors of your soul.

V

Willow is you. Fresh you are. Like the sweet
  fragrance of a handful of flowers picked
with gleeful countenance and universal oblivion.

VI

Unfortunate it is when such beauty withers
  superseded by odours of expiration. Such
is inevitable. One fails to alter the inevitable course of
  death that our lives take.

VII

Willow, you and I are passing strangers who
  have gazed within the orbits of each other's
eyes. A spark has been ignited within my immoral
  being. Your elusiveness is but a thorn that I am
not able to expel. Therefore, let me love you
  with equally elusiveness. Like a hidden cloister that
must undoubtedly maintain anonymity.

VIII

Lucky is the one who has the privilege to lovingly
    kiss and touch your precious eyes. Willow, be
happy that in this big old cold world a being exists who
    thinks of you. Is it worth the revelation of the
being's identity? I will anticipate your answer: No!

IX

Pleasure is mine if you accept my poetic stanzas
    without reproaching me in thought. It is not
my intention to offend but to provoke awareness
    of my esteem for you. My elusive willow
that one must never grasp.

Speak Beyond All Consequences

I

If there is a logical justification in divulging one's inner thoughts
then speak. In apprehension be silent,
Safe guard yourself from boulders, why? There is no guarantee
that the one you pursue will know the meaning of gratitude
or recognition. Can I tolerate rejection? Answer: If
I have been to hell, suffered; faced spiritual death;
I will be bold.

II

Impulsive presumption has its way like a supernatural
force. Like a demon it possesses your mind rendering
you irresponsible for your actions. Reality, rationality becomes
secondary, subdued as irrational hearts say there are
no boundaries to adhere to. Divulge your feelings regardless
of the consequences.

III

My gender was and is still made to feel awfully guilt-stricken,
    labelled indecently if she dares to accost you. Some
still see it as absurd to woo a man. It is out of the social
    norm, unacceptable. But if you are open-minded you will
understand that this old brute of a world is capable of
    much change. The reversal of roles is undoubtedly
apparent.

IV

Hell, you have made such an impact on my mind. You plague
    me. I fail to prevent myself from thinking about you, so
What if you love someone else. Even if you should never find
    out who I am, I will feel better for my divulgence. I
will feel relieved that you are very much aware that you
    are loved.

V

I am beginning to wish I had never seen your lovely
    face. Eyes can be dangerous. Should I darken my
receptive mirrors so that I should never see another
    perfectly structured face as yours? To shield myself
I would like to idealistically glide blindfolded through life
    lacking all emotions. I don't want to be able to cry,
love, hate or experience pain. I wish I was a cold
    unfeeling stone. Safe! Then I would be resilient
when I look you in the eyes. I would be exempt from
    love and pain.

VI

Coming back to reality I appreciate the fact that to
    love is to be alive. To be alive and not be loved
is a waste of the body. To be not alone and to be
    with someone without love is to die. I guess
I am fortunate to be capable of showing genuine
    human emotions. Love is a rarity these days,
very few fall in that category. Sometimes I feel
    the world is void of love. I am alive!

VII

Do you hate me with abundance? or do you think crazy!
  absurd! stop! no more! forgive me for my
divulgence, as the song says: If language were
  liquid it would come rushing in. Instead here we
are in a silence more eloquent than words could
  ever be.

VIII

I would like to hold your hand and lead you through
  the sweltering streets of Spanish Town and through
the streets of Florence. Chase you with sand in my
  hand to throw at you on the sandy beach of
Ochi Rios. Then come to rest on the Venetian steps
  of the Rialto Bridge. I would fall into your arms
and while holding you I would kiss and touch your
  precious eyes without any intention of letting
you go. I would ask you to hold me like an infant
  that refuses to rest.

IX

Listener of woes is what you are. And I demand
nothing of you. If it is fate that we should
meet I will say: Hello friend, you have consoled
me once, and with pleasure you became my
sustenance which preserved my integrity through
the darkness. Goodbye, I shall not intrude again.

A Scream Within

It came like a blatant slap
An echo was heard saying: told you so,
up against a brick wall, punch and
punch but there is no way out.

Restrictions, restrictions are the biggest
impediment. Bureaucracy strongly
enforces its boundaries like a vicious
bear with sharp claws.

Discontent engulfs and shines like
Crimson polished nails. Solitude
reinforces its stronghold, pen and paper
show how invaluable their skills are.
In manipulation they express the scream
within.

There is your bed now lie down on it. That's
not easy to accomplish as integrity is
being attacked. Too restless to adhere to
that.

A voice in the distance screams: go on take
it on the chin, keep you guard up, go through
the motions. Keep on thumping that
brick wall, kick it too, find a hammer
hit back at life, but never lie down on
that assumed bed.

Time You Old Culprit

I
Will you always be around indefinitely? I esteem your elusiveness. No one has ever seen you slip away except on the clock's face. The wind is felt but not seen, if it is strong enough it causes havoc and so do you.

II
We earthly beings have the same disease in common: ageism. Time, you old culprit, you were there when my mother nurtured me in her womb, when she gave birth to me. You are everywhere.

III
Your watchful presence haunts me and inseparably declines. You wipe youth away and replace it with rapid deterioration. Sickness and pain contort, In forty years I will not recognise the real me.

IV

Will you suck the moisture out of my body and leave me dry? Or will you give me a timeless appearance? It is not for you to really decide because I don't think you are in control of yourself.

V

Let's sit a while and play cards. You be the dealer and deal me a good hand, let me have goodness in my last days, let me escape the fate of what is inevitable by early expiration. Time, you old culprit, dance with me.

Anticipation

Life is a mystery – one that can be compared to a mere box of chocolates.

The first layer has been spoiled by heat.

The bottom layer is untouched and is in perfect condition.

Time please lend an ear. Tell me is my life really cursed?

If not can I expect success in years to come?

Will I have the opportunity to be comfortable?

Will I love God as I do now? Will I be harassed by life?

Will I continue to be?

They say time is the greatest story teller. Let's wait and see.

Reminiscence

I held you in my arms as you alone conversed in
baby gibberish. I cared for you and loved you.

Your illness frightened us. I remember when your
legs were swollen and we thought you had
polio. Fortunately that was an unfounded scare.

Now your gait is so elegant, you are as tall
as a coconut tree. Young, strong and supple
in limbs, you are life itself in innocence.

In pastoral calm you are clinging close to
nature, the most natural source. You are
wise to avoid confrontation with this sepulchre
of a world.

Read your Bible, that is your sustenance of life,
it is your spiritual foundation, a stepping stone
from this world to the next.

Plough the barren field and sow the seeds
of wisdom, let it yield its fruits to nourish
and comfort your delicate soul.

Let our Father be your guide and walk side
by side with you to meet the bright star that
illuminates the entrance to the next inevitable dimension.

Disarray

At the ending of each year empty souls parade
with well wishes. They shout at mere strangers:
Merry Christmas and a Happy New Year. Is
Christmas the only time to smile and wish
others well?

I heard such wishes as last year passed me
by and wondered if my new year would be
prosperous. Indeed, I prayed that it
would be good. Three-quarters of the year
has passed like a whirlwind leaving broken
bones and disarray.

I want to pick up the disarray and straighten
the mess but my exhausted body tells me no,
Rest a while, rest a while.

I only feel strong and alive when I take myself
out of this stalemate decay. There are days when
I wake up and open the curtains
to see the snow on the rooftops
and would like to venture out, but as the day passes
I become impeded by my own thoughts:
go back to bed, rest a while, rest a while.

Mixed Feelings

A weary soul who had climbed thousands of mountains
in two decades spied in anguish a form dangling
upside down, pink in colour and struggling to scream
at life. Unappealing features caught the eyes of
the aching weary soul.

Love at first sight was not experienced. Disappointment
took hold and superseded that. The worn-out soul gasped
with disbelief and could not relate to imperfection.
The resemblance did not belong as it turned away
and pulled the covers over its weary existence.

Since then they have engaged in Spartan battles,
Disappointment has become the catalyst to the soul's
aggression. At one time it was hoped that the
passive being would assert itself.

Instead passivity allowed the stronger yet weary
force to trample it into the ground. You smile and
declare that you love your persecutor but deep
within your soul you are severely injured. Passivity's
wounds are stitched with profound suppressed
hate. Please divulge your inclinations before
you explode.

Away from its clutches passivity is like a free bird
in flight above the clouds and all are pleased
for you to develop a self, your own individuality.

If passivity's thoughts could be read, I can imagine that
it would be thinking: poor decadent soul, in
earnest, I have no contempt for you, but mere pity
for your imprisonment in your loathsome friendless
solitude.

If you had the holy spirit of goodness abiding in
your perishing carcass it would be easy to escape your
bitter lot.

Let the anger and unforgiving flow out
of your veins. Instead let love and goodness
smile as they take you by the hand and say:
open, you cold heart and love the defenceless
form who dangled and pierced the silence
of the sterile and immaculate environment two
decades ago.

Last Resort

Conscience counsels against irrationality.
But the serpent hoodwinks: yes here I am,
hide your face in the mire of unmentioned
deeds.

The dawn breaks, chores begin, uninhibited
stares beckon without the need for verbal
exchanges.

Yes, they are lacking sustenance, don't sit
still. Survivors know that they must be
nourished regularly.

How can you say they are beautiful when
eyes, souls are empty with excruciating
bitter biting hunger.

Minds misfunction, disorientation sets in.
Cupboards are bare. Rooms are cold and
void of a morsel of comfort. The clock
ticks the cursed hours away, and the telephone
doesn't ring any more.

Reassurance enters unseen and whispers in a
calming tone: hush, the cupboards will be
filled, each and every room will be warmed
and the glow in your hearts will be
replenished. The telephone will ring, wait a while, be
patient.

A figure in its last resort opened the door and
ventured out into the darkness of the night
where promises must be accomplished.

Dear Lord

Once I had the holy spirit within
    But now it seems to be gone
        Anger seems to have replaced it
            I try desperately hard to hold on to the spirit
                but it is so difficult.

Love your neighbour as you love yourself the
    Good Book says. But how can you when
        the people you meet from day to day
            insult you and try to trample you
                into the ground?

Anger rages within me because I cannot lie down
    and be trampled upon. At the same time I am
        not worthy to be a Christian, who can
            only be pure if living according
                to Bible principles. Turn the other cheek.

I am angry with myself for failing God, and I am
　angry at myself for not being able to
　　Love my persecutors. Dear life, dear Lord,
　　　let me learn to be tolerant and
　　　　less sensitive, because if I
　　　　　fail to achieve these qualities
　　　　　　I am sure to punch
　　　　　　　someone.

Band of Gold

A band of gold was placed upon his finger when certain vows were made in haste.

Within, a tiny seed of life grew. A being stood meagre with anguish in its soul as it was led to the slaughter.

A moment before the journey commenced, bitter brutal verbal exchanges took place: I wish that seed was not implanted in you.

Had it not been so, there would not be a purpose to wait here in the icy early hours of the morning for the internal imprisonment in your band of gold.

The being is pleased that life within has progressed into a rosebud that secretly brings precious joy. He who felt imprisoned has expired into oblivion although the unrested soul has continued to wander the entire house.

Independently, separate lives are lived but that rosebud does not take sides because it gives love in abundance to those at war.
As never-ending battles of anguish express hate and claw at each other. Get out, will you! Get out! Get out!

Time stands still, because nothing happens, he doesn't go, the haunting continues – at least until he is surprised by the fact that the locks on the doors are changed.

Feelings

Anger burns within a perishing being
who tries to suppress it.

Adrenaline flows and flows, within
it pours and pours.

Within the being the adrenaline eats
at its stomach.

It eats at it like lime or salt
which has been poured into an open
wound.

The being wants it to stop but it can feel its
pituitary gland in its head.

It sends signals to its pancreas to
flood its veins with the anger and pain
it has no wish to experience.

It was victorious in argument, but yet
it has come away. Persecuting itself
with the painful biting adrenaline.

You should have said this, you should
have said that.

It goes on and on for nights and days,
weeks and many months. Is it worry
– or what?

Fresh Flowers and a Wreath

The reality of his absence struck me today.
"I am indeed in mourning," I said as I got up
and made my way to the door with burning
tears in my eyes.

Send me fresh flowers and a wreath so I can be
sure he is no longer here.

I will go back to the house we once shared in
love, anger, hate and reconciliation.

The room that once contained his belongings
stands empty and cold. When I look on the
ground I can see his bed that is no longer there.

Send me fresh flowers and a wreath so I can be sure
he is no longer here.

I can hear him strumming on his guitar in solitude,
the guitar which I bought as a surprise for him.
It now stands idle on my photograph table.

Send me fresh flowers and a wreath so I can
be sure he is no longer here.

It wounds like a knife as I think about him,
as I exist in my numb state of mind. I have
tried very hard to say I did not love him but I
did. When I listen to the records that he bought
for me, and when I see the paintings he got for
me I die inside.

Send me fresh flowers and a wreath so I can
be sure he is no longer here.
Send me, send me flowers and a wreath so I can be sure
that he is dead.

Boundaries

They say we do not try to integrate but when we do
they reject us. Their cold stares and their reticence
speak louder than words.

If you see your white colleague on the street, he or
she may try to avoid you. If not, a quick 'hello'
and a dash for the station will be their way of
escaping your company.

They make it quite clear that it's all right to mingle
with your own and not the other. Certain
boundaries must not be crossed even if you
want to, as they will not permit you to do
so easily.

Like Cheshire cats their beautiful cold smiles
will bombard you, but they will quite often occupy
the chair which is not adjacent to yours.

You are a good decent person with confidence, and
to receive such treatment makes you wonder
who has the disease.

Social pressures stab you in the guts if you love a
white man who loves you in return. As you walk
hand in hand down the street, all of a sudden
you are the centre of the wrong type of
attraction.

The most hateful glares are hurled at you
by people who do not know you. Caught like
a rat in a trap in a battle of hate, you decide
that love is stronger than anything in terms
of feelings that we are capable of. Therefore,
we should step beyond the boundaries and be united
in love and peace. Only the strongest can
survive in this harsh old world.

The Blues

They sang the blues and their opposers found it contemptible.

Their anguish poured out into musical tones as facts were divulged. Billie sang of Southern trees bearing strange fruits, blood on the leaves and at the roots.

Nina sang 'Mississippi God damn!' The men sang and strummed on their guitars, they told of love, tragedy, politics and whatever anguish ailed them.

Bronzy was inquisitive and wanted to know what kind of man Jesus was.

Freedom was sought in their pleas, from the nightmarish hell they found themselves enslaved in, some wanted a band of angels to carry them home in sweet exaltation.

They sang the blues and their opposers found it contemptible.

But why is it that now their opposers have come to recognise jazz and the blues and exploited it for their own ends?

Could the answer be greed?

Gold Coast

You are the land of the people with their beautiful stature. They stand tall and they walk proudly on.

To perceive your features is akin to a priceless diamond that many pillagers have died for.

Willow and fresh you are like a light breeze upon a pleasant spring morning.

Where are you tonight? Do you think of me, the way I recollect my brief encounter with you? Maybe yes, maybe no. Perhaps I shall never know.

Let me stand beside you and smell the freshness of your clean intellectual body.

Let me touch your soft hair and your lovely
strong features. You are indeed a magnet which
draws my attention to my initial homeland – the
place from where my forefathers were snatched.
Tell me of your culture which I have been denied.
Let me beat out my profound frustrations on the drums
of my ancestors until I find sweet blessed peace
– or is that an illusion?

The walls within the walls of the host culture
suck my spirit and spit it into an abyss. If I
was in the company of my people wouldn't you
agree that my cheeks would bloom with love, pride
and unity?

A Gaze

Silence conveys much inclination
and I am able to know its meaning.

Your gaze is piercing, it bombards me
and at the same time it is so reassuring.

It tells me that admiration and desires
are inseparable: uncertainty and
optimism also walk hand in hand.

I reciprocate your vision, yet that
conscience of mine says, go not beyond
a gaze.

Smart and beautiful you are, diligent
too. Are you kind, honest, gentle, sincere
and warm – unattached?

You see, if the answer were yes, I may still
be reluctant to go beyond an admiring
gaze.

Caution whispers: Once bitten twice shy.